LUK in SRI LANKA

Written by Srianjali Gunasena
Illustrated by Nuria Lamsdorff

THE TRAVELS OF LUK

Text © Srianjali Gunasena
Illustrations © Nuria Lamsdorff
Printed in Sri Lanka by M.D.GUNASENA AND COMPANY PRINTERS (PRIVATE) LIMITED
Third Edition 2018
ISBN 978-955-44588-0-2

Published by Srianjali Gunasena & Nuria Lamsdorff

INDEX

This is my journey, my name is Luk;
I travel far and wide.
A sprinkle of magic is all you need
To join me for the ride.

I close my eyes, keep very still,
Whisper the name in my mind.
Clap 3 times, then shout out loud,
"Sri Lanka" is the place I find!

1

Come with me, adventurous friends,
To explore a land far away.
Where crickets nest in palmy fronds,
And leopard cubs wrestle and play.

The world is at our fingertips,
A magic place to live.
Let's learn from different cultures,
And see what we can give.

Sri Lanka

Pt. Pedro
Kankesanthurai
Jaffna
Elephant Pass
Kilinochchi
Mullaitivu
Talaimannar
Mankulam
Mannar
Aruvi Aru
Vavuniya
Yan Oya
Nilaveli
Trincomalee
Wilpattu
National park
Anuradhapura
Kalpitiya
Kala Oya
Puttalam
Sigiriya
Polonnaruwa
Pasekudah bay
Dambulla
Maduru Oya
Kalkudah bay
Wasgomuwa
National park
Batticaloa
Deduru Oya
Mahaweli Ganga
Chilaw
Maduru Oya
National park
Kurunegala
Matale
Maya Oya
Kandy
Negombo
Kegalla
Peradeniya
Botanical garden
Ampara
Gal Oya
Gampaha
Gal Oya
National park
COLOMBO
Kelani Ganga
Nuwara Eliya
Badulla
Avissawella
Pottuvil
Hatton
Ella
Monaragala
Arugam bay
Mt. Lavinia
Horton Plains
Ratnapura
Kalu Ganga
Kalutara
Uda Walawe
National park
Yala National park
Bentota
Sinharaja
Rain forest
Walawe Ganga
Kirindi Oya
Kataragama
Tissamaharama
Hikkaduwa
Hambantota
Galle
Unawatuna
Matara
Tangalle
Welligama
Mirissa

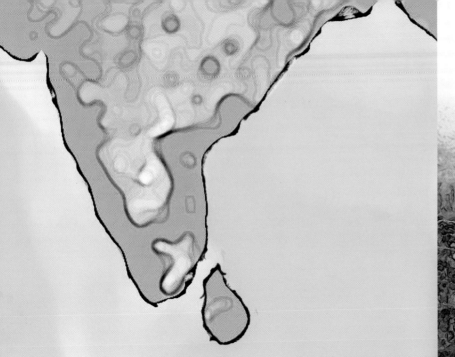

The Island of Sri Lanka,
A tear drop in the sea.

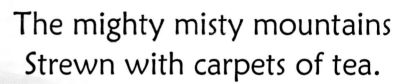

The mighty misty mountains
Strewn with carpets of tea.

Lush canopies of jungle,
The leopards and the bears.

The beaches and their waves,
Surf them if you dare.

I meet a leopard upon my way;
He offers me his paw.
"I'll show you around this magic land
That you've not seen before."

4

There are many ways to travel,
All through the day and night.
Feel the wind in a tuk tuk;
Make sure you hold on tight!

The overloaded buses
Rush through crowded streets.
There's no time for dawdling,
They have passengers to meet.

The roads are sometimes scary,
Dodging cows and bikes.
Whizzing round the bends
Gives both of us a fright!

6

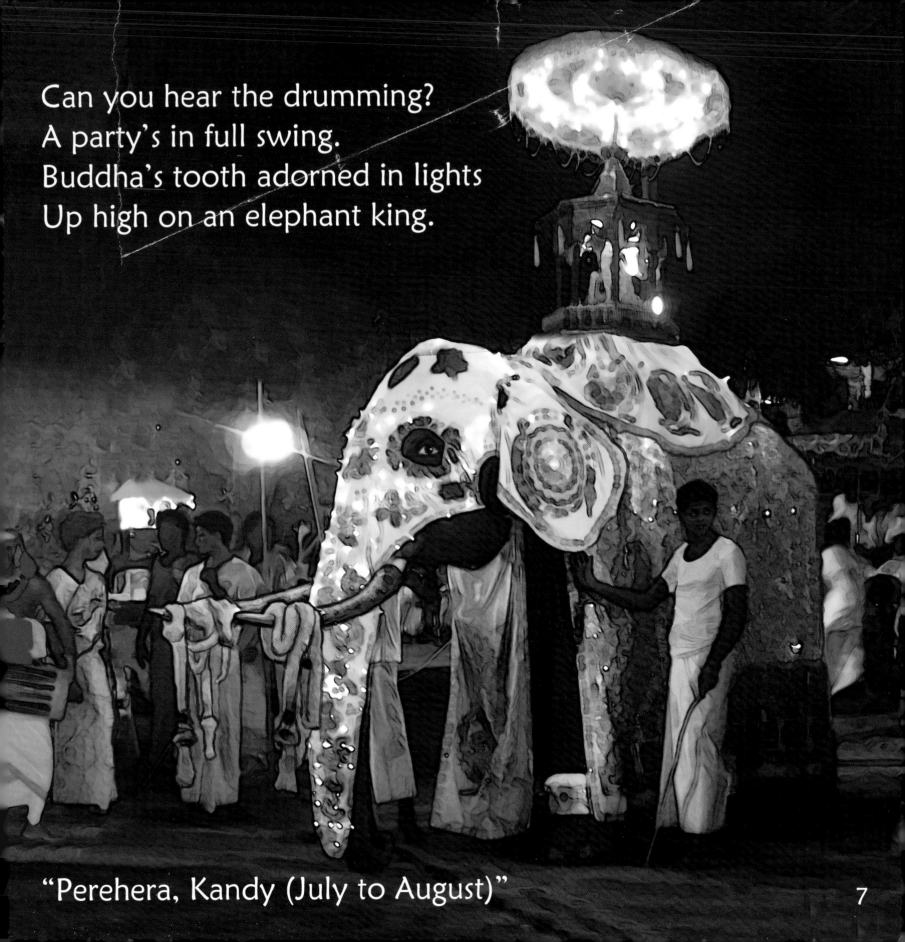

Can you hear the drumming?
A party's in full swing.
Buddha's tooth adorned in lights
Up high on an elephant king.

"Perehera, Kandy (July to August)"

7

The dancers are flashing white and red,
The drummers quicken their beat.
See the procession weave its thread
Through the cheering street.

The Kandy train clatters and clicks,
It winds through hills so high.
Children on their way to school
Turn to wave goodbye.

9

We spy a mountain through a clearing.
"Let's try and climb to the peak!"
We pass an old man, tired and frail,
His body thin and weak.

"Sri Pada, also called Adam's Peak"

"My life's dream is to reach the top."
His voice is husky and dry.
"Even when it seems too hard,
Failure is failing to try."

On hearing this I search around
For something to give the man.
"A walking stick will help you finish,
I'm so sure you can!"

11

The view from the top is outstanding.
We can see for miles and miles.
There's a tear in the old man's eye,
On his face, a great big smile.

We find a room to rest our legs,
A pillow to lay my head.
I climb into the mosquito net,
To keep me safe in bed.

13

The morning starts with a brilliant shine,
We venture outside to look.
Carpets of tea is all we see
In every valley and nook.

The tea pluckers heave their loads,
All day they toil in the heat,
To bring to us the finest leaves;
Ceylon tea - you just can't beat!

14

My friend and I enter a cave,
We blink in the faded light.
Surrounded by statues of Buddha,
What a magnificent sight!

"Dambulla" 15

"Let's climb this rock" says Leopard.
"There are beautiful paintings from old.
In the site of an ancient palace,
 Where stories of kings are told."

"Sigiriya"

Coming down, the leopard stumbles,
Trips on a fallen stone.
"Ouch, my leg is in such pain,
I think I've broken a bone!"

17

Hearing these cries, a woman appears,
She bends to have a look.
"Don't worry leopard, you'll be fine,"
And she opens a big old book.

18   "Ayurvedic medicine"

"For a graze, burn or cut on your foot
I'll make a turmeric paste.
If you feel queasy in your tummy,
Ginger tea you must taste.

For the common sniffly cold or flu
Digest some pepper and spice.
To quench your thirst - King Coconut,
It tastes so sweet and nice."

19

The gentle lady wraps his paw
And takes the swelling down.
Soon he is up and walking,
So we journey into town.

Look at the graceful ladies,
In saris all styles and shades.
Rose and turquoise, pink and blue,
Purples, magentas and jades.

21

I learn to tie a sarong,
It suits the tropical sun.
I'm glad I wore my underpants
In case it comes undone.

We're on a safari adventure.
At the river we stop to see,
A herd of wild elephants
Splashing the water with glee.

We arrive in a crumbling city,
Once home to kings and preachers.
This is the ancient capital,
Now over-run with creatures.

The animals feel quite at home
Amongst the pillars and trees.
Spot the mongoose and the snake;
What others can you see?

"Anuradhapura"

24

Under the shade of the Bodhi tree
Is a place to be quiet and still.
A chance for you to meditate,
Sit down, relax and chill!

25

We follow the elephants to the north
And wade through shallow lagoons,
To reach a city where temples shimmer
Under the brightest full moon

26   "Jaffna & Elephant Pass"

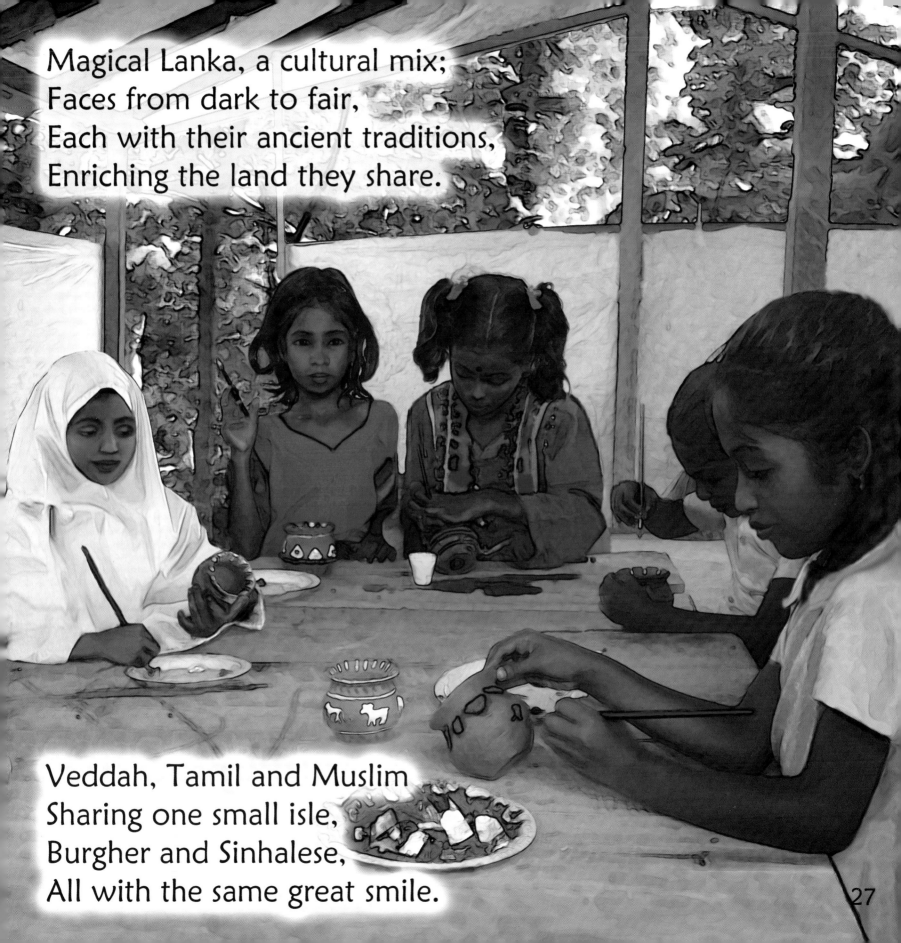

Magical Lanka, a cultural mix;
Faces from dark to fair,
Each with their ancient traditions,
Enriching the land they share.

Veddah, Tamil and Muslim
Sharing one small isle,
Burgher and Sinhalese,
All with the same great smile.

27

"Have you tried speaking?" asks Leopard.
"Some Sri Lankans are tri-lingual.
Try to speak some greeting words,
It will make your tongue tingle!

ஆயுபோவன்
"Ayubowan" (sinhala)
வணக்கம்
"Vanakkam" (tamil)

"Ayubowan or Vanakkam
Is hello and welcome too.
Isthuthi, or nandri
If you want to say thank you."

28

All this travelling makes me hot.
"Follow me," says leopard "I know!"
He fills a bucket from a well,
And soaks me head to toe!

The glassy waters of Trinco
Are perfect to snorkel and dive.
The magnificent natural port
Makes it worth the drive.

"Trincomalee"

30

We go to visit Swami rock,
Also called Lover's Leap.
History says there's a temple,
Lying in the sea so deep.

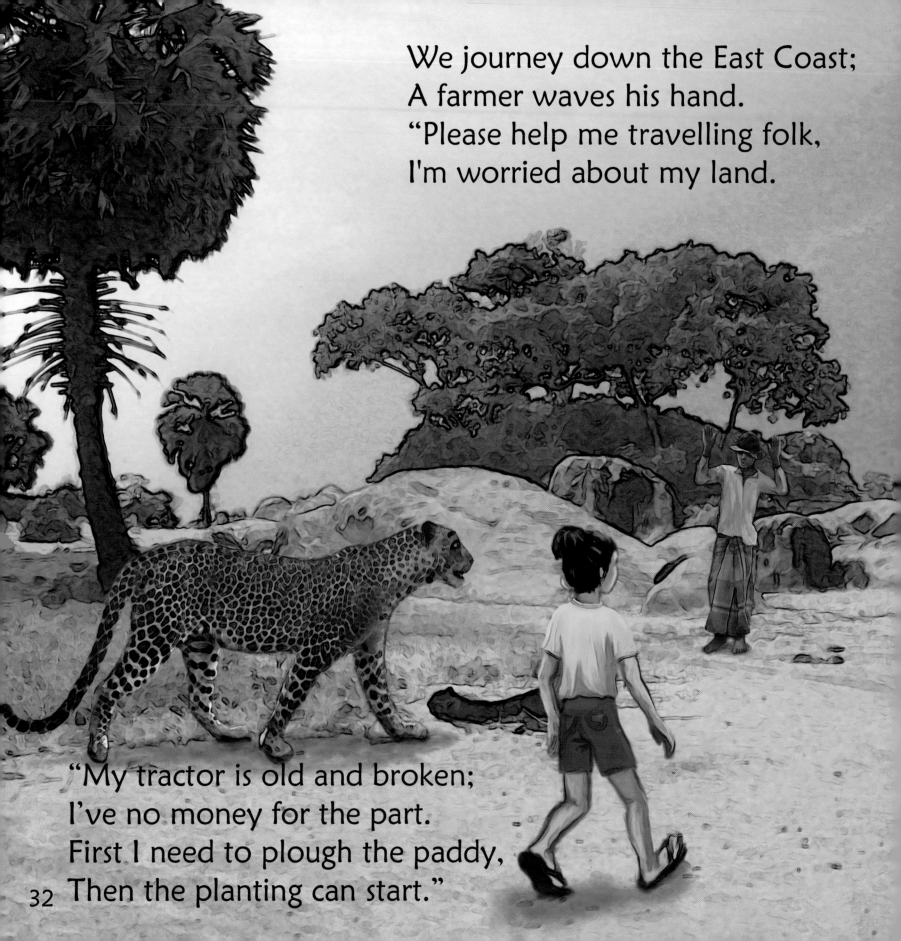

We journey down the East Coast;
A farmer waves his hand.
"Please help me travelling folk,
I'm worried about my land.

"My tractor is old and broken;
I've no money for the part.
First I need to plough the paddy,
Then the planting can start."

32

A buffalo grazing on the water's edge
Has some time to spare.
"Don't worry," he calls, raising his head
"It's work we all can share."

We push the plough to the paddy field,
Pulled by the noble beast.
When we are done, the happy farmer
Invites us all for a feast.

"Sweet and sour sambols,
Creamy curd and honey;
Explosions on your taste buds,
Comfort in your tummy.

"String hoppers on your plate,
Soak up coconut curry.
Relax and peel a sweet banana,
Take your time, don't hurry."

36

Mangosteen

Coconut

Sour orange

Banana

Woodapple

Rambutan

Guava

Passion fruit

"Plump, purple mangosteen,
Sticky woodapple jam.
Which fruit do you like best?
Try them all if you can!"

Lime

Pineapple

Mango

Water melon

Papaya

37

They use their fingers, not a fork,
To eat their rice and curry.
Mix it, ball it, pop it in;
If you make a mess don't worry!

"I need to use the toilet,"
I whisper to my guide.
"Squat down over the hole,
Don't sit!" the leopard confides.

39

Instead of paper I wash with water,
A bucket and jug nearby.
I give my bum a wriggle and jiggle,
It doesn't take long to drip dry.

40

We say goodbye to the farmer
And head to Arugam Bay.
Relax on the beach, splash in the waves;
What a wonderful day!

41

The thunder clears its mighty throat,
The bright blue sky turns black.
The heavy monsoon sheds its load,
With a click, a crash and a clack.

42

The storm passes, the boats set out
To collect their catch from the sea:
Lobster, seer fish, tuna and prawns,
What a scrumptious dinner there'll be.

43

See the surfers ride the waves,
What a thrilling place to be.
The wild water froths and bubbles
In the glistening glittering sea.

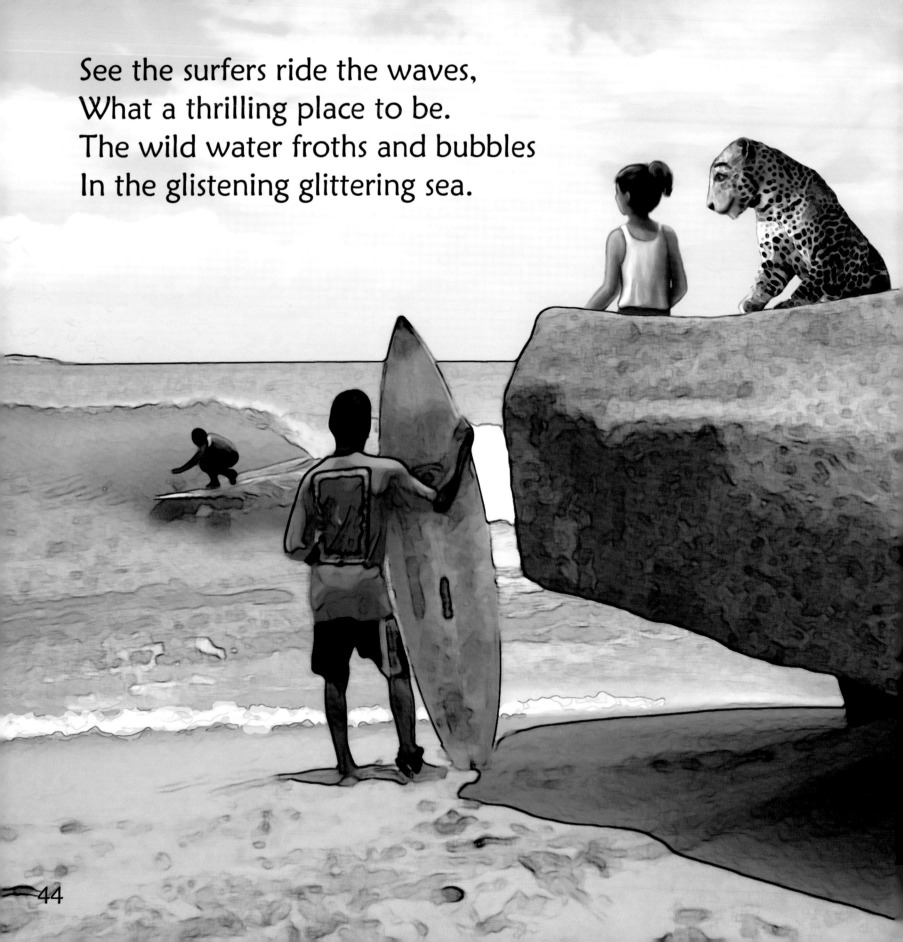

The ball spins high in the air,
As we watch a game of cricket.
The fielder rushes to catch it;
The batsman sprints to the wicket.

Leopard shows me where he lives,
"My home is Yala East.
Keep very quiet and you will hear
The sound of every beast."

Oh the majestic elephant,
Weaving through the trees;
Lifting up her mighty trunk
To munch the juicy leaves.

46

There's the hungry crocodile,
Slyly stalking his prey.
Don't come near the water's edge;
You'll surely make his day!

If you walk through the jungle,
So bravely late at night,
Be wary of my leopard friends;
When hunting they might bite.

We follow petals blowing in the wind
And stumble upon a wedding.
An elephant dressed as a warrior prince;
The groom no less a king!

49

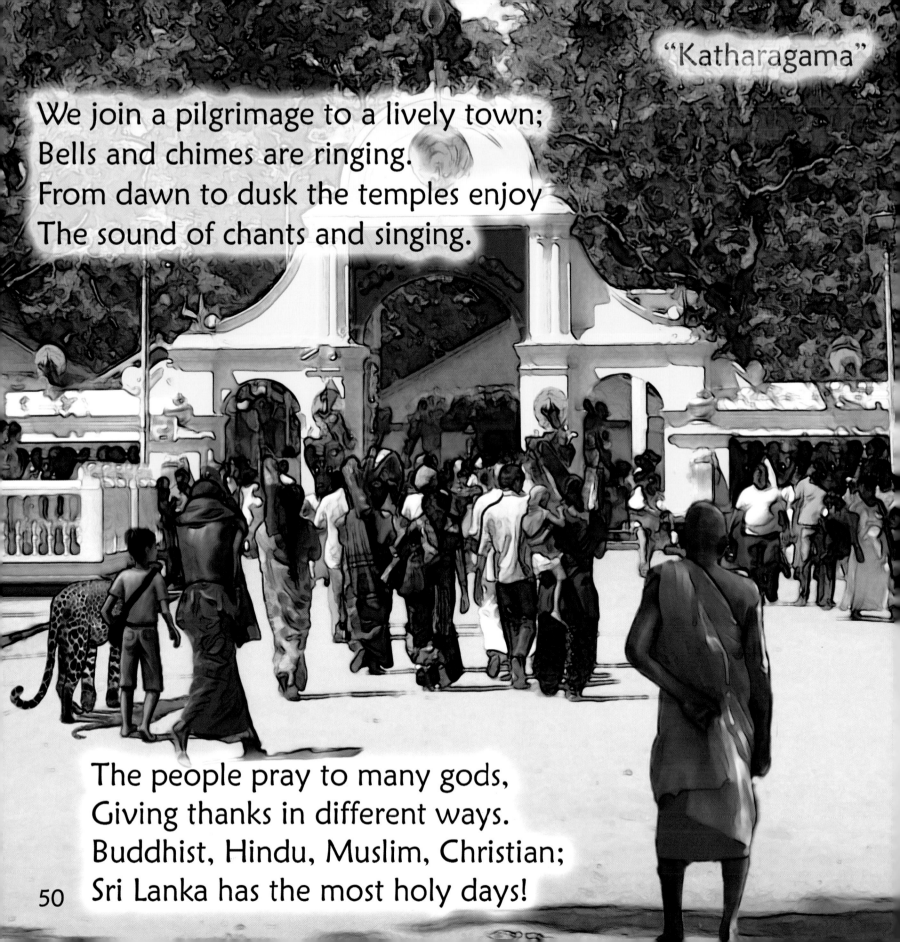

"Katharagama"

We join a pilgrimage to a lively town;
Bells and chimes are ringing.
From dawn to dusk the temples enjoy
The sound of chants and singing.

The people pray to many gods,
Giving thanks in different ways.
Buddhist, Hindu, Muslim, Christian;
Sri Lanka has the most holy days!

A beautiful forest surrounds us;
I bathe in a crystal pool.
A waterfall gushes from mountains high,
The ultimate way to be cool!

"Sinharaja Rainforest"

51

We travel the southern beaches
To snorkel amongst the reef.
A chance to meet a giant turtle
Although it may be brief.

"Hikkaduwa"

52

Up the west coast we go
To the most wonderous sight;
Dolphins and whales gliding around
And jumping with all their might.

"Kalpitiya"

53

"I've had a great time," says leopard,
"And now we'll say goodbye.
Be true to your life's journey;
Have fun and don't be shy."

I say farewell to my special friend,
Who shared with me each mile.
A marvelous guide to this magical land;
We hug and our hearts smile!

54

I think about how lucky I am
To have such a wonderful friend.
These words are the leopard's parting gift
To take to my journey's end.

"Tiptoe through the jungle,
Leave only foot prints in the sand,
Respect Sri Lanka's creatures
And their precious, precious land."

I raise my eyes towards the sky
Listening to the words on the wind.
I loved my Sri Lankan adventure;
Where will my next journey begin?